Beavers For Kids

Amazing Animal Books for Young Readers

By John Davidson

Mendon Cottage Books

JD-Biz Publishing

Read More Amazing Animal Books

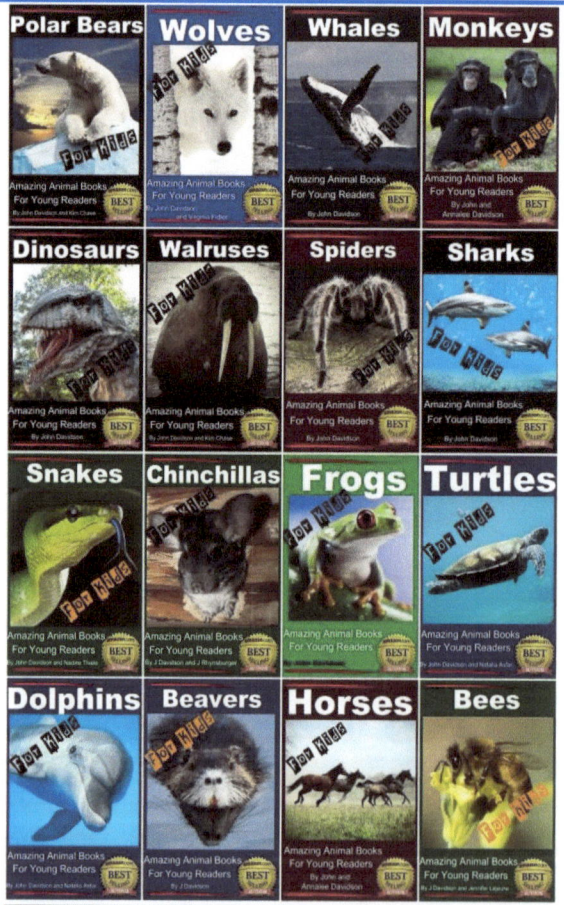

Purchase at Amazon.com

Table of Contents

1. Facts About Beavers

Evidently, the beavers are very interesting species that can captivate everyone to try and know more about them. Here we have noted down some really interesting facts about beavers.

Beavers are herbivores and primarily nocturnal as they are more active at night. They have weak eye sight but make up for it with strong hearing and sense of smell. They are semi aquatic but tend to be slower while on the ground. There are two known species of beavers around the world, the North American beaver and the Eurasian beaver both of which interestingly enough never mix with each other.

The young ones of beavers are called kits during the first year and yearling during the second. They are social and live in colonies of several beaver families. A typical beaver family consists of a male and female with around 2 to 4 kits.

The Canadian national animal, beaver is also depicted on their five cent piece and even feature on the 1849 pictorial stamp. Ironically, in Canada once the beaver was almost hunted to extinction due to the love for its fur.

Swimming comes naturally to the beavers and they are brilliant at swimming and can even hold their breath under water for more than 15 minutes. This trait helps them evade some of the predators easily.

The beavers have a very unique alarming system which used to alert other members of their colony in the region. When under threat beavers successively dive into water while forcefully slapping their broad tail into it. Amazingly, the impact is pretty loud and audible over and under water to great distances serving an alarm to other beavers around.

Beavers are quite an amazing member of the rodent clan, the second largest in the species to be precise. Already they have made a name for themselves as 'builders', it is because they are known to have the characteristics of making dams over streams and rivers.

The beavers have teeth which keep growing all through their lifetime. These are used to cut the trees and build dams.

Surely some of the above facts about beavers were not known to you till today.

2. Beavers

Beavers are nocturnal members of the rodent family. These curious animals are large rodents that have sharp teeth and wide flat tails. This large, semi-aquatic animal is best known for the dams they build. While living in groups called colonies the beaver uses the water to help protect themselves from larger predators. Their behavior fits the name 'busy as a beaver' as they work to create a calm pool for them to live in.

These mammals are known for gnawing trees in less than suitable areas to help them create their dams. This habitat while not perfect for other animals will make a wonderful home for this talented water dweller. With the aid of their strong, sharp teeth the beaver will take down trees and place them in the water to form pools. That trait makes the beaver similar to humans in the fact that they change their environment to suit their needs.

In the world of the beaver the homes they have created with their tree removal and placement are known as lodges that will house the colony. The entrances to their lodges are normally situated in the middle of their new pool and will be underwater to add a touch of security for these semi-aquatic animals. The beaver is a plant eater and must rely on the safety of their lodge to keep them from harm.

This amazing animal has the ability to swim at a pace of 5 miles per hour, an ability to remain underwater for as long as 15 minutes and have eyelids that work like tiny swimming goggles giving the ability to see underwater. The oily fur that covers their body works as a water proof bathing suit. In the animal kingdom the beaver is the craftsman often creating ponds where other animals are in need of water to drink.

3. Beaver Tails

The beaver has one of the most special tails in the animal kingdom and uses this tail in a number of ways. The beaver tail is different from many other tails because it is a long and flat tail. The tail is usually a foot and a half long, half a foot wide, and has very little fur on it. The tail of the beaver is actually closer to being scaly like a dragon than it is a furry tail.

Beaver Tail

A beaver tail is very important to the beaver since it provides a way to keep balance while on land while the beaver is standing to chew through tree trunks. Beavers also use their tail as a sort of cushion if they do fall down. This means the tail is not only a balancing support, but a form of protection as well. Beavers use their tail to act as a warning system to their neighbor beavers too. They will smack their wide, flat tail onto nearby water to make a loud slapping noise. This lets other beavers around them know there is danger in the area.

Beavers use their tail like a rudder while swimming, allowing them to steer themselves like a ship would without having to slow down in the water. Having a huge tail acting as a rudder lets some beavers swim as fast as five miles an hour in the water, which is pretty fast for an animal that waddles around on land. The tail of a beaver acts like a personal air conditioner. The tail stores some of the beaver's body fat and lets the beaver release body heat when it needs to cool down.

Even though having a wide, flat would seem good for smacking down mud on a dam, beavers do not use their tail for this. Beaver tails are actually very delicate, and are made of the same materials the human nose is. Try to remember all the good things a beaver tail does for the beaver the next time you think about our rodent friend.

Muskrat

Sometimes people mistake muskrats for beaver but a muskrat is smaller and has a round tail.

4. Beaver Dams

A beaver dam is the intertwined mix of trees that have been gnawed down by a colony of beavers. The large rodent animal will begin their dam with the placement of trees or poles across the water vertically, that structure will be continued as the beaver adds trees horizontally. Their new construction will become a dam as fantastic mammals stuff all the gaps between the trees with roots, mud and weeds to prevent the water from passing. In the building of their dam the beaver is often known to construct canals for the water to run so that their cut down trees are easier to move to the location of the new dam.

This new dam will be the starting point for the beaver to build their home or lodge. It will stop the water from moving and result in a new pond. Their dam construction process will continue until there is plenty of water around the lodge. That is how this aquatic animal protects themselves.

Through the use of their strong teeth the beaver will gnaw at trees in the same way a chainsaw works, until the tree falls for future placement in their dam. As the water raises within the new pond the beaver will have created a safe environment for their colony to live. This log jam soon becomes a beaver dam and will change the way the area was before the pond was built.

While the dam is filled with moss, weeds and trees this smart beaver will also place trees that can be used as a food source later when other sources of food are not available. Their beaver dams make the perfect addition to their safety, provide deeper water for their lodges, and allow for the winter storage of food supplies all within their pond.

5. Beavers Habitat

Beavers are large rodents which can be mistaken for big rats at a distance. They are very cheeky, industrious and tenacious semi-aquatic mammals. This means that they live partly in water and on land; however they spend most of their time in water. They have a slow movement on land but can be really fast when frightened, in water they are excellent swimmers which is facilitated by their body adaptation. They have large, paddle-like, flat tails with webbed rear feet which enable them to swiftly propel their bodies in the water. They have a lifespan of between 12 to 15 years but at times live up to a maximum of 20 years.

Beavers live in lodges which they build near pond of water or even dams. In the absence of dams, beavers are known to construct their own dams by placing vertical poles which are crisscrossed with horizontal branches and the gaps filled with mud. Due to their engineering nature, beavers can easily construct a dam that surrounds the entire lodge. Beavers can also be found in banks of rivers and streams. They dig deeper into the banks and use this as stores for foods such as hay, corn stocks, cattails and tree limbs. These holes are along the water beds near the source of food and the lodge mostly under the Maple trees or other hardwoods.

Beaver eating a grass by the lake in Yellowstone

Beavers can stay in the water without resurfacing for up to fifteen minutes. They have very transparent eyelids which serve as goggles in the water. They have an underwater entrance into their lodges that are not visible to other animals and predators mostly at the middle of the pond. The lodges are subdivided for the various family members and they have a drying are where the beavers dry themselves when they come out of the water. The beavers habitat is surely an interesting one to study on as it unveils the great skill that they posses.

6. Beaver Houses

Beavers are the best gnawing animal and it is the second biggest rodent. They can live for about 16 years and there are different types of beavers like Elbe, polish, Scandinavian, Canadian, Ural, Rhone, Mongolian, Newfoundland, golden bellied. Their colonies made more than one dams to offer deep water to safeguard against predators and to build material and floating food. The population of beaver is also decline because of huge hunting. People hunt for fur, glands availed as perfume or medicine.

Beaver lodge in early Spring

Beaver houses are known as a lodge. It can be 10 to 20 feet and eight feet above the water. Beaver houses can contain two to five entrances, they are open under water hence the beaver can enter the lodge below the winter ice. Containing the entrance underwater safeguards them from predators. The house of beaver is made by using logs, sticks, dry leaves and mud. It is also built on the banks of a river or a pond. Within one week a beaver family can make a dam which is have been noted were above 1,000 feet long. Dams are designed from birch, aspen, mud or willow trees. Beavers which live on flat areas certain times create waterways known as canals hence they can get heavy branches and trees to their house by not using their teeth.

Beaver dams are made like a protection against wolves, coyotes and bears. They work at night time and they are professional builders, carrying stones and mud with their teeth. Due to this reason, damaging a beaver house without eliminating the beaver is impossible. Beavers can also rebuild these kinds of dams in one night. Certain bigger beaver houses contain more than one partition. For the apartments generally have no communication except by water. The lodge contains underwater entrances to create the entry highly hard for other animals.

7. What Beavers Eat

Beavers are second largest rodents living in the world and are famous for building dams, canals, and homes. These are nocturnal creatures and their native town is North America and Eurasia. The north American species is called Castor Canadaens and the Eurasian species is known as Castor fiber. Beavers have become endangered species as they are often hunted for fur.

Although, they have weak eye sight, their other senses are very powerful. The largest tools of beavers are their sharp upper and lower incisors which they use to cut barks or even fell trees for the purpose of building dams. The tail of beaver is big and flat which it uses both on land and water. In water, it uses to warn other beavers from predators and on land it uses as a prop to sit, stand or counterbalance.

Eating habits of beavers are very interesting. Just glance at what beavers eat:
Beavers are herbivores and survive solely on eating aquatic vegetation. Their favorite plants are herbaceous plants like clover and raspberry canes. As these are semi-aquatic species, these even love to eat all kinds of aquatic plants. Beavers also enjoy eating leaves of aspen, cottonwood, birch, alder, dogwood and willow trees. With their powerful front teeth, they eat barks of certain trees. Actually these rodents chew the barks of larger trees to sharpen their main tool - teeth. These also love to eat roots, shoots, and tender branches of herbaceous plants.

The American beavers are very fond of water lilies, cattails, sedges, etc. Although, they are semi aquatic species, they do not eat fish or other aquatic animals. As these rodents do not hibernate, they pile their food stock for winters. They store sticks underwater and survive on these sticks when the pond freezes. They live underwater for the whole winter and nibble on the sticks that they have stored.

Beavers are hardworking and brilliant engineers and can construct beautiful dams by using trees.

8. Trapping Beavers

Beaver trapping was actually a major industry over 100 years ago in America. For about 300 years in The United States and Canada fur trading was a major industry. It was actually one of the earliest and most important industries in North America and helped to develop the country.

Fur trappers that ventured across the country trapping beavers for their pelts to make hats and stoles that were popular with the wealthy in Europe at that time, and these men helped to map the country during their explorations. Fur trappers met the Native Americans and developed trade with them and established relationships with them that help them live in the wild.

Native Americans would trap beavers and trade their pelts to the fur traders for tools and implements that they could not make themselves like steel knives and firearms, and decorative beads for making jewelry and clothing. Europeans that lived in the wilderness and trapped were called mountain men because they spent so much time in the mountains.

These days not much fur trapping goes on in America, but there is some. Most fur trapping for trade happens in Canada. Most of the time in America when someone wants to trap a beaver, it's because the beaver is damaging their land. Beavers are the only animal besides man that makes a dramatic change to their environment.

Which provides habitat for the beaver and other wildlife. The beavers along with fish and turtles live in the water, and deer and bears and other animals use the lake to drink from.

A lot of the time when someone traps a beaver now, they trap them in a no-kill trap that is designed to catch the beaver without hurting it. This way, they can move the beaver to another location where it can live happy and free, chewing down trees and building dams.

Publisher

JD-Biz Corp

P O Box 374

Mendon, Utah 84325

http://www.jd-biz.com/

Mendon Cottage Books
P O Box 374, Mendon Utah 84325

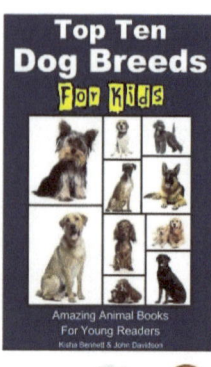

Top Ten Dog Breeds For Kids
Amazing Animal Books For Young Readers
Krista Bennett & John Davidson

German Shepherds
Dog Books for Kids
K. Bennett

Bulldogs
Dog Books for Kids
K. Bennett

Dachshund
Dog Books for Kids
K. Bennett

Poodles
Dog Books for Kids
K. Bennett

Labrador Retrievers
Dog Books for Kids
K. Bennett

Rottweilers
Dog Books for Kids
K. Bennett

Boxers
Dog Books for Kids
K. Bennett

Golden Retrievers
Dog Books for Kids
K. Bennett

Puppies
Dog Books For Kids
Amazing Animal Books
By John Davidson

Beagles
Dog Books for Kids
K. Bennett

Yorkshire Terriers
Dog Books for Kids
K. Bennett

Dogs Top Ten Dog Breeds For Kids
Amazing Animal Books For Young Readers
Zahra Jazeel & John Davidson

Cats For Kids
Amazing Animal Books For Young Readers
K. Bennett & John Davidson

Foxes For Kids
Amazing Animal Books For Young Readers
Zahra Jazeel & John Davidson

Wolves For Kids
Amazing Animal Books For Young Readers
By John Davidson and Virginia Fidler

Monkeys

Amazing Animal Books
For Young Readers
By John and
Annalee Davidson

Whales

Amazing Animal Books
For Young Readers
By John Davidson

Kittens

Amazing Animal Books
For Young Readers
By John Davidson

Meerkats
For Kids

Amazing Animal Books
For Young Readers
John Davidson and Lisa Barry

Elephants
For Kids

Amazing Animal Books
For Young Readers
Kim Chase & John Davidson

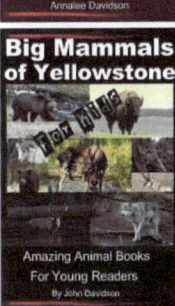
**Big Mammals
of Yellowstone**

Amazing Animal Books
For Young Readers
By John Davidson

Big Cats
For Kids

Amazing Animal Books
For Young Readers
By John Davidson

**My First Book About
Pandas**

Amazing Animal Books
By Annalee and John Davidson
BEST
Children's Picture Books

Chinchillas

Amazing Animal Books
For Young Readers
John Davidson and Jannie Rhynsburger

Beavers
For Kids

Amazing Animal Books
For Young Readers
By J Davidson

Bees

Amazing Animal Books
For Young Readers
By J Davidson and Jennifer Lejeune

**Animals of
Australia**

Amazing Animal Books
For Young Readers
By John Davidson
and Shawn Vincent Wilson

Frogs
For Kids

Amazing Animal Books
For Young Readers
By John Davidson

**My First Book About
Frogs**

Amazing Animal Books
By John Davidson
Children's Picture Books

Tigers
For Kids

Amazing Animal Books
For Young Readers
Kim Chase & John Davidson

Scorpions
For Kids

Amazing Animal Books
For Young Readers
John Davidson

Snakes
For Kids

Amazing Animal Books
For Young Readers
By John Davidson and Nadine Thiele

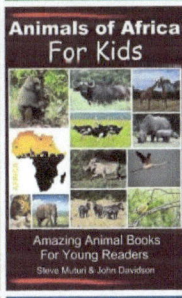
Animals of Africa
For Kids

Amazing Animal Books
For Young Readers
Steve Muduri & John Davidson

Dinosaurs
For Kids

Amazing Animal Books
For Young Readers
By John Davidson

Sharks
For Kids

Amazing Animal Books
For Young Readers
By John Davidson

Spiders
For Kids

Amazing Animal Books
For Young Readers
By John Davidson

**Giant Panda
Bears**
For Kids

Amazing Animal Books
For Young Readers
By John Davidson

Giraffes
For Kids

Amazing Animal Books
For Young Readers
Valeria Arcas & John Davidson

Eagles

Amazing Animal Books
For Young Readers
Nicholas Williams & John Davidson
For Kids

Bears
For Kids

Amazing Animal Books
For Young Readers
Zahra Jazeel & John Davidson

Download Free Books!
http://MendonCottageBooks.com